8 Things to Do When You Receive an

IRS

Notice

Vincent W. Davis

LAW OFFICES of
VINCENT W. DAVIS
& ASSOCIATES
Eliminating Injustice

ISBN-13: 978-1511859615
ISBN-10: 151185961X

DISCLAIMER

This publication is intended to be informational only. No legal advice is being given, and no attorney-client relationship is intended to be created by reading this material. If you are facing legal issues, whether criminal or civil, seek professional legal counsel to get your questions answered.

Law Offices of Vincent W. Davis & Associates
150 N. Santa Anita Ave., Ste. 200
Arcadia, CA 91006

1-888-888-6582

Offices in:

Arcadia	Beverly Hills	Irvine
La Mirada	Long Beach	Los Angeles
Ontario	Riverside	Woodland Hills

CONTENTS

8 Things You Need to Do When You Receive an IRS Notice

Introduction

It is estimated that the Internal Revenue Service will contact millions and millions of people annually to audit personal and business tax returns, and collect taxes which the IRS perceives are owed. If you are one of those individuals, keep calm, don't panic. It is not the end of the world.

The best thing to do is begin to educate yourself about the issues. Do not procrastinate and ignore the IRS. Things will just get worse, not better.

This book will give you some general guidelines and explain some of the general procedures to rely on when the IRS contacts you about your personal or business matters. It is not meant to be an all-inclusive tax law or tax procedure treatise. The purpose of the book is actually to give you a 30 thousand foot overview of the process and what you should do next.

Primarily, you should be contacting a tax professional. There are many competent professionals who can assist you during this stressful period. In my opinion, at the top are the tax lawyers. Every tax lawyer is not the same. You want to find one that has an expertise in Tax Resolution. Then there are the Certified Public Accounts (CPA's); and every CPA is not the same. Some CPA's are proficient in financial auditing, business consulting, tax planning, tax preparation, and so on. But for this purpose, you'd probably be better off with a CPA who specializes in Tax Resolution work. Then there are the Enrolled Agents (EA), again the same is true. You want an EA who specializes in Tax Resolution work.

I hope this book gives you the overview, which will help you remain calm. After all, knowledge is power. The more power you have, the better you will be able to resolve your tax issues.

1. Identifying the type of letter you received

The IRS will usually send notices to you if they are reviewing, examining, or processing any activity on an account. An account is the IRS information under a social security number (SSN) or Employer Identification number (EIN). There are many reasons why the IRS would send out a notice, but for the purpose of tax resolution, the ones that we should be on the look-out for are:

Collection Notices

Audit/Examination Notices

Tax Lien Notices

Non-Compliance Notices

Some people decide that not opening an IRS notice will just delay the process, but that is very far from true. You always want to open any notice you receive from the IRS to understand what they may be requesting or what they are reviewing and why.

The most common of notices that we see are collection notices. It is important to identify which collection notice you have received. The IRS sends out a sequence of collection notices before they actually start the collection process of levies and garnishments. So, it is good to identify what those letters look like. Thoroughly reading the notice is always a good idea.

Another way to identify what letter you have received is by the notice code, usually located on the top right and/or bottom right of the notice. The initial collection letter you will see is a CP 71, which states the current liability owed for the year listed.

There are a few other notices that follow this one before the IRS actually takes any collection action. The ones to look out for, and be very cautious about, are:

Notices CP 504/CP 90 and

Letter 1058(LT 11)/ CP 91

The notices CP 504 and CP 90 are the notices preceding the final notice. CP 504 and CP 90 state that if the full balance or a payment arrangement is not met 30 days from the date of the notices, the IRS will pursue wage and bank levies, seize property and can file a federal tax lien on the year(s) listed on the notice.

The notice will say **"URGENT"** in large bold letters at the top of the notice. The IRS will not take collection action until a final notice has been sent, unless they have previously sent all of the sequential letters including a final notice. If the final notice (1058/CP 91) was already sent out in the past, all the IRS would need to send is another CP 504 to pursue collection again.

An example of this happening is if a taxpayer, who was previously in collections, set up an installment agreement and later defaulted on the agreement. At this point, the IRS will pursue collection action again. Identifying a final notice is simple as it will state:

"Call immediately to prevent property loss, final notice of intent to levy and notice of your right to a hearing"

in large bold writing at the top of the letter. It basically states the same as the CP 504 except that this is the last notice you will receive before the IRS takes action. It also states that one has 30 days, from the date on the notice, to pay the entire balance off or make a payment arrangement for the year(s) listed. If a taxpayer takes no action within those 30 days, the IRS can start the levy process against one's wage and bank accounts - and also file a federal tax levy under that taxpayer's social security number. The CP 91 is also a final notice but states that the IRS will levy up to 15% of social security benefits.

Other notices to watch for are:

Form 668 (Notice of federal tax lien),

CP 2000 and
CP 3219/Letter 531-T
(notice of deficiency)

Form 668 is a notice stating that the IRS has filed a federal tax lien under your social security number, and it will state what year is included in the lien. This could impact you greatly or may not impact you much at all. It all depends of what you plan to do in the near future.

A federal tax lien will mostly impact your credit and can have negative affects when you try to qualify for a loan. Financial institutions would rather not do business with someone with a federal tax lien. This can prevent you from purchasing a vehicle or a home.

A federal tax lien can also affect one's employment or business. Some employers will run one's credit as part of the background check to verify if one is a qualified candidate for a job position. Also, a taxpayer that owns a business may have a problem obtaining credit from suppliers for his/her business.

A CP 2000 is a notice sent to a taxpayer when the IRS has determined that what they have on file, and what a taxpayer is reporting on a tax return, do not match. This could cause an increase or decrease of tax.

CP 3219/Letter 531-T is a notice of deficiency. This is basically the same as notice CP 2000, except this notice has a proposed amount and states how the amount was calculated.

2. Understanding What the IRS Wants

It is always a good idea to have a licensed tax professional review any notice you don't understand, but sometimes - most of the time – the notices are self-explanatory. First, it is always important to understand why you have received an IRS notice. Second, recognizing if you need to take any action is very important, especially if a deadline needs to be met. Third, it is very important to know how to respond or what documents to provide if it is necessary to do so.

Understanding IRS notices can be as simple as making a payment for a balance owed or as complicated as reviewing a notice of deficiency and trying to figure out how the IRS came up with their proposed assessment. If you know that you owe for a particular year, and you have the means to pay the balance (without it causing much financial strain), it is always best to pay off the balance before incurring more interest.

But, if you find yourself in a tough financial position, and you have no means to resolve the issue, it is always a good idea to consult with a tax professional and find out what options are available to you.

It's also helpful to read the entire notice and fully understand why you have received a notice in the first place. If it is a reminder notice of a balance owed, it will have information on how to pay the debt. And, like a reminder notice, a collection notice will always ask you to pay the balance immediately, but the collection notice will inform you of the consequences of not paying the balance. There are so many reasons for receiving a notice, but you can always visit the IRS website to get further clarification before making a call to your tax professional.

Recognizing if any action is needed after receiving an IRS notice is always very important. Sometimes no action is needed; like when receiving a notice that a refund has been applied to previous balance, or that the IRS has received and accepted your amended return. There are times when you will need to provide documentation or give a statement on an examination or review being performed by the IRS. There are times when a revenue officer is assigned and they are demanding certain documentation to verify a means to collect on a liability owed. If you find yourself in a position like this, it is always a good idea to seek representation. Handling a case like this on your own can get very complicated.

Understanding what documents you need to provide to the IRS is very important. Knowing what documents are needed can be the difference between clearing up the issue and complicating it more. Sometimes you may have to amend a tax return to clear up an issue, or sometimes you may need to seek guidance to perform a payment plan or settlement with the IRS, sometimes both. Knowing the process and what documents will be required is always crucial to getting the best results possible.

3. Contacting a Tax Professional for Clarification

It is always a good idea to have a licensed tax professional review any notice you don't understand. If you receive an audit notice, such as a notice of deficiency, this could be very difficult to understand. Sometimes it is difficult to understand how they came up with an assessment or why you have been selected for and audit examination, even if it is sometimes a random selection.

Other notices can be from a revenue officer asking for certain documentation, and you are unsure what exactly that is. Sometimes a notice is asking for a telephone or an in-person conference, and you are not sure if you should attend, and/or what you need to provide. In these cases, it is always a good idea to consult with a tax professional and seek representation.

4. Verifying Your Alleged Liability

When receiving a collection notice, you need to understand why you are receiving this notice. Knowing what you should (or can do) is the next step. Also, if you have a question on what options you have available to you, it is best to consult with a tax professional to guide you through the process and provide the best results allowed by law.

The next step after receiving a collection

notice is always the most important step. You need to determine if you are liable for the balance due. It can be as simple as going through your records and identifying the issue. If you don't have access to all of your records, or if you cannot determine how to resolve this issue, this can be a difficult task to take on. There are several options for resolving this, but the process - and the right guidance - can have a tremendous impact on the result.

A tax professional can always help with verifying the issue, explaining the step-by-step process, and guiding you through the 43wolu5ion of this issue. Staying in compliance with the IRS is always crucial to one's life, as they can be very aggressive in the process of collecting on a debt owed. This can cause much personal and financial stress to you and your loved ones.

The tax professional will gather transcripts from the IRS detailing the actions that have taken place for any given year. He/she will determine whether you are in filing compliance and where you stand in the collections process. Your balance can be in notice status, with the Automated Collection System (ACS) or with a

Revenue Officer. If your account is in Notice Status, this means that all balance due notices and initial collection notices have been issued, but no actual collection activity has taken place. If your account is with ACS, this means your account is with the collection department - and levies are imminent. When an account is with a Revenue Officer, all account activity and communication must be handled directly with this individual.

5. Understanding Your Options

A tax professional can assist you in determining what your next steps are. A professional can help you understand the collection process and the options available to you. They will communicate with the IRS on your behalf and gather information or documentation that will assist in the resolution process. They will ask about your history with the IRS, and the circumstances that caused the tax liability.

The tax professional will gather transcripts from the IRS detailing the actions that have taken place for any given year. They will determine whether you are in filing compliance and where you stand in the collections process. Your balance can be in Notice Status, with the Automated Collection System (ACS) or with a Revenue Officer. If your account is in Notice Status this means balance due notices and initial collection notices have been issued, but no actual collection activity has taken place. If your account is with ACS, this means your account is with the collection department and levies are imminent. When an account is with a Revenue Officer, all account activity and communication must be handled directly with this individual.

If the tax professional has determined that the taxpayer is in filing compliance, the resolution process may move forward. If a taxpayer is not in filing compliance, arrangements must be made to ensure the missing returns are filed as soon as possible. This may also include filing original returns for returns previously filed by the IRS and/or amending prior returns. During this time the professional will communicate with the IRS to inform them of the steps taken by the taxpayer to resolve their issue. A tax professional can communicate with the IRS to prevent collection action.

6. Proposing a Payment Plan

Setting up a monthly installment agreement with the IRS is always a good way to get back in compliance with the IRS. But what if you can't afford the monthly payment they are proposing? If you contact the IRS directly, they will ask you what you can afford to pay on a monthly basis. Sometimes they won't accept your proposal if they feel it is too low. You need to know what options you have. The IRS will only ask for a full payment – one time or in installments. In these situations you will need to contact a tax professional to assist you with this matter and explain how this issue can be resolved.

If the tax professional has determined that the taxpayer is in filing compliance, the resolution process may move forward. If a taxpayer is not in filing compliance, arrangements must be made to ensure the missing returns are filed as soon as possible. This may also include filing original returns for returns previously filed by the IRS and/or amending prior returns. During this time the professional will communicate with the IRS to inform them of the steps taken by the taxpayer to resolve their issue. A tax professional can communicate with the IRS to prevent collection action.

There are options available for you to resolve the liability. You can set up an Installment Agreement based on a financial analysis, submit an Offer in Compromise, or request a Currently Non-Collectible Status. Any of these options is based on eligibility. A tax professional will be able to determine what to do based on a thorough financial analysis. Even a lower monthly payment plan can be determined if the financial analysis shows this to be an option.

7. Knowing Your Right to Protest

When receiving an IRS notice with a tax liability or proposed assessment, you need to understand why you are receiving this notice. Knowing what you should or can do is the next step. Also, if you have questions on what options you have available to you, it is best to consult with a tax professional to guide you through the process and provide the best results allowed by law. If you are not sure you are liable for the amount owed, but don't know how to go about proving this, a tax professional can assess the situation and identify what is needed to resolve the issue.

The best way to approach this situation is to contact a tax professional with experience in dealing with these issues. If the account is not in collections, you will need to contact the number on the notice and verify to whom you should address the issue. If the account is in collections, you will need to get in contact with the automated collections department (ACS) and speak to a representative who can assist you. If a revenue officer is assigned to the case, this will be the individual who will the point of contact for the case. Knowing your rights is always crucial to the case since the IRS is not always willing to hear out a person trying to prove they are not liable for a debt. Remember, if you don't know your rights, you don't have any.

You should know you have a right to appeal a determination made by a department or individual at the IRS. Knowing when that is available, and when you should exercise this right, is important as well. Also, you have the ability to address your concerns to the taxpayer advocate department if you feel you have not been given a fair attempt to address your questions and concerns. The taxpayer advocate department is another resource that may be helpful in understanding and resolving your tax issue(s), but it is always important to know when you should exercise this right. Keep in mind everything you provide and state will be documented under your IRS account and can be viewed by any IRS department.

8. Proving it with Documentation

It is never a good feeling to check your mailbox and find a tax bill in your name. There are times that the IRS does make mistakes or doesn't have all the information at their disposal. In these cases, knowing what you will need to present or explain can give you the result you are looking for. Knowing what you should and shouldn't provide can make a huge difference. You don't want to end up providing something that wasn't needed and having the IRS question other areas of your finances. A tax professional will assist and guide you through this process and will review all your documents before submitting them. A tax professional will be able to help you sort out the right documentation to present to the IRS, with the right explanation, to provide the best result possible.

A tax professional will also know how to prepare and present the documents to your advantage. Disputing a liability is not only about the documentation provided but also the manner in which it is presented to the IRS. The presentation can be the determining factor in successful audit reconsideration.

There is also the matter of successfully communicating and negotiating with an auditor. A tax professional is not only experienced in IRS negotiations, he/she will not be intimidated by a revenue agent the way a taxpayer may be.

Summary

When you receive a notice from the IRS, it is important to know what to do. If you do or say the wrong thing, it could be very stressful, and it could cost you thousands.

Just as you would not want to wander through the Amazon jungle without an expert guide, it can stressful and unproductive to wander through the IRS jungle without an expert tax professional. Remember, saving a few dollars by doing it yourself could cost you thousands of dollars in taxes and penalties.

Tax Attorney – tax attorneys can give legal advice, CPA's and enrolled agents can't

Certified Public Accountant (CPA) – prepares tax returns; represents you in front of the IRS; can help you when you get letters or notices from the IRS.

Enrolled Agent – can do the same thing as a CPA, but they haven't gone to school to get an accounting degree, and they haven't passed the Certified Public Accountant's test. They have taken an "enrolled agents" test.

I have not included an ordinary tax preparer on the list, because their jobs are limited to putting your information on tax forms and filing the forms with the IRS and State tax authorities. They can rarely help you beyond that.

In my experience, an enrolled agent is probably better for tax resolution problems. In this particular realm of tax resolution, an enrolled agent is not necessarily cheaper than a CPA.

However, if you think you need legal advice, your best result will be achieved with a tax attorney.

www.ingramcontent.com/pod-product-compliance
Lightning Source LLC
Chambersburg PA
CBHW070927180526
45168CB00005B/2183